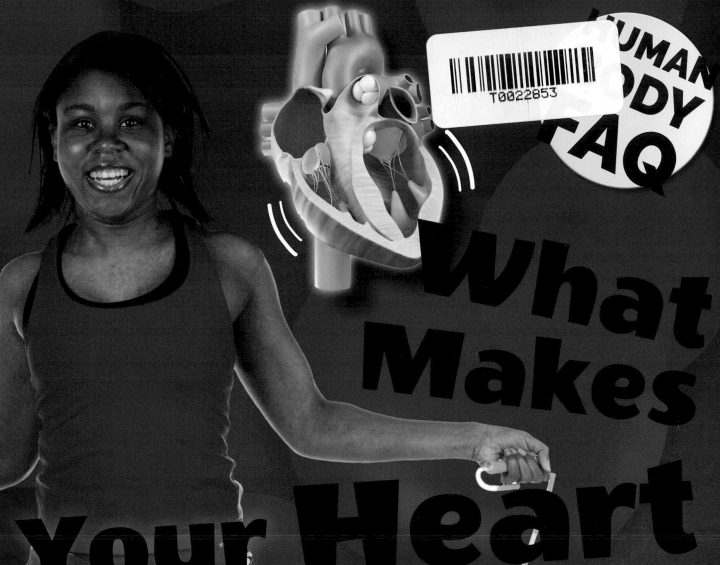

HUMAN BODY FAQ

What Makes Your Heart Beat Faster?

Questions About Internal Organs

by **Thomas Canavan**

PowerKiDS press

Published in 2017 by **The Rosen Publishing Group, Inc.**
29 East 21st Street, New York, NY 10010

Cataloging-in-Publication Data

Names: Canavan, Thomas.
Title: What makes your heart beat faster? / Thomas Canavan.
Description: New York : PowerKids Press, 2017. | Series: Human body FAQ | Includes index.
Identifiers: ISBN 9781499431704 (pbk.) | ISBN 9781499432251 (library bound) |
  ISBN 9781499431728 (6 pack)
Subjects: LCSH: Cardiovascular system--Juvenile literature. | Organs (Anatomy)--Juvenile literature.
Classification: LCC QP103.C317 2017 | DDC 612.1--dc23

Designers: Supriya Sahai and Emma Randall
Editors: Joe Harris, Anna Brett and Lisa Regan
Cover design: Paul Oakley

Picture credits: Cover illustration: Shutterstock. Interior illustrations: Shutterstock

Manufactured in the United States of America
CPSIA Compliance Information: Batch #BW17PK: For Further Information contact Rosen Publishing, New York, New York at 1-800-237-9932.

Contents

What is a human organ?

Doctors define organs as collections of tissue formed in a special way to perform particular jobs. There are lots of bodily tasks to be done, and your organs help you do them. Different organs make sense of the world around you, turn food into fuel, send nutrients to where they're needed, and get rid of things that are unhealthy.

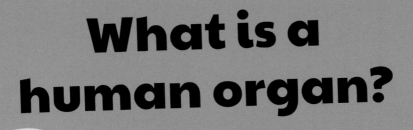

Is your eye an organ?

Yes! It is an organ that reacts to light to allow you to see. It is less developed in babies; they only see black and white to begin with.

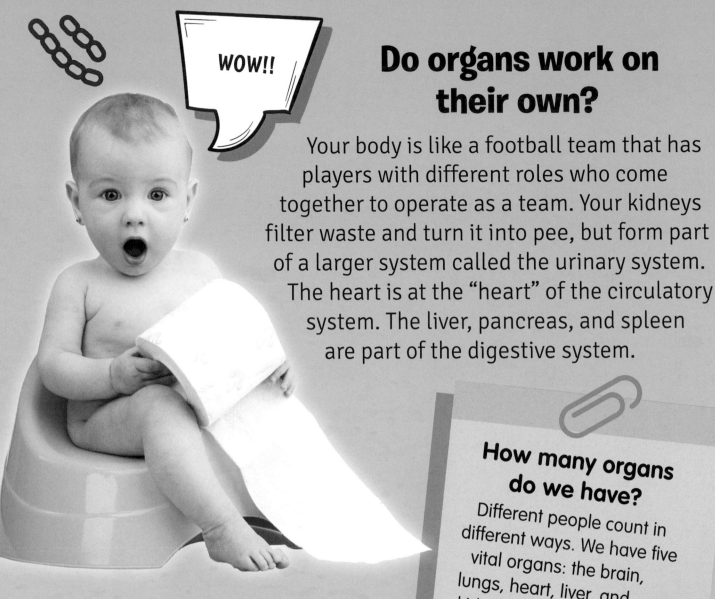

WOW!!

Do organs work on their own?

Your body is like a football team that has players with different roles who come together to operate as a team. Your kidneys filter waste and turn it into pee, but form part of a larger system called the urinary system. The heart is at the "heart" of the circulatory system. The liver, pancreas, and spleen are part of the digestive system.

How many organs do we have?

Different people count in different ways. We have five vital organs: the brain, lungs, heart, liver, and kidneys, and around 70 others.

Are we born with all our organs?

Our organs form in the months before we are born, so from day one we have a complete set. Some of them, such as the heart, lungs, and liver, have already been working hard. Others, such as the reproductive organs, develop more fully when we are older.

Why does your brain take control?

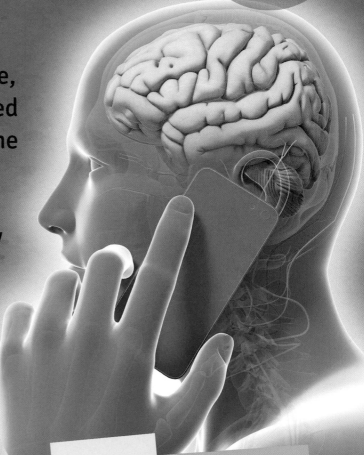

Keep thinking that your body is like a team. To be effective, the players (human organs) need to work together. They follow the orders of the coach who has an overview of everything. Your brain is like a coach, constantly observing what's happening and sending out orders to the rest of the body.

Some images, known as optical illusions, can trick the brain.

Does the brain ever get mixed up?

Sometimes your brain receives confusing information and processes it in the best way it can. In an optical illusion like this one, too many bright patterns mean the brain can't process the image. It appears to be spinning on the page.

How does your brain control things?

Your brain can tell which area of your body needs a boost and calls on other areas to help out. If you're exercising really hard, for example, you need more oxygen near your leg muscles. Your brain gets your lungs and heart to work that much harder.

Is there such a thing as "brain food"?

Certain foods are good for your brain. Fish, nuts, broccoli, avocado, and—wait for it—small amounts of dark chocolate can improve memory, learning, and concentration skills.

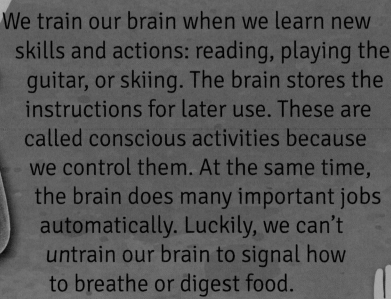

What can we train our brain to do?

We train our brain when we learn new skills and actions: reading, playing the guitar, or skiing. The brain stores the instructions for later use. These are called conscious activities because we control them. At the same time, the brain does many important jobs automatically. Luckily, we can't untrain our brain to signal how to breathe or digest food.

How does the heart work?

Your heart is a pump that pushes oxygen-rich blood to every corner of your body. To begin with, blood flows in and fills the right side of the heart. This blood is then pushed around to the lungs where it picks up oxygen. The oxygen-rich blood then flows back into the left side of the heart and with a strong, sharp pump it is sent out of the heart and off around the body.

Aorta (to body) 10

Left pulmonary artery (to left lung) 5

Superior vena cava (from upper body) 1

Left pulmonary veins (from left lung) 6

Right pulmonary artery (to right lung) 5

9   4

Left atrium

Right pulmonary veins (from right lung) 6

7

Left ventricle

2

Right atrium

Right ventricle

Inferior vena cava (from lower body) 1

How many times does your heart beat each day?

Your heart beats around 100,000 times a day and about 35 million times a year.

What is a pulse rate?

Your pulse is the beat of your heart. You can sometimes feel your heart beating through your chest but to count the beats properly you can measure your pulse. Press two fingers onto the inside of your wrist and count the beats for 15 seconds. Multiply this number by four to get your pulse rate, which is measured in beats per minute.

How big is your heart?

Close your hand into a fist shape—that's the size of your heart. Once you stop growing so does your heart.

Why does your heart pump twice?

Blood has to first be pumped into the heart where it fills the atria, and then it has to be pumped out of the heart and around the body via the ventricles. That's why each heartbeat is actually two pumps.

How much blood does your heart pump?

An adult body has at least 1.2 gallons (4 l) of blood, which carries oxygen and essential chemicals to every part of the body so that muscles and organs work properly. The blood completes the return journey from those parts, carrying waste. In order to move this amount of blood all the time, you need a strong, reliable pump—your heart.

How much blood is that in a lifetime?

Your heart is made up of two pumps, with extra-strong muscles squeezing them in a rhythm. Your heartbeat—the number of squeezes—is about 90 per minute. With 2.5 billion beats in a typical lifetime, that's the same as your heart moving enough blood to fill 100 Olympic swimming pools.

Rusty!!!

How far does blood travel?

The human body contains over 60,000 miles (96,000 km) of blood vessels. Blood cells travel along these highways and byways many times every day!

Why does blood look red?

The blood moving around your body contains varying amounts of oxygen. This reacts with an iron-rich protein in your red blood cells, turning it red—just as iron turns rusty red when it meets oxygen in the air. Blood with lots of oxygen is bright red, and gets darker as it releases the oxygen around the body. Some creatures, such as spiders and lobsters, have copper instead of iron in their blood, making it blue.

I'm feeling a bit blue...

Why do veins look blue?

On pale-skinned people, the veins close to the surface look blue, not red. They still contain red blood, but they appear blue because of the way light travels through the skin.

Why is it hard to hold your breath?

It starts to hurt if you try to hold your breath for too long. That's your brain telling you to let your lungs do their work. It's their job to get the oxygen from each breath in, and get rid of carbon dioxide and other wastes when you exhale. You need your lungs to provide the breath for moving, speaking, singing, and laughing.

Hmphhh...

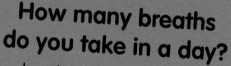

How many breaths do you take in a day?
In a typical day, you will breathe in (and out again!) more than 20,000 times.

Do your lungs have muscles?

Your lungs can't breathe without help. And that help comes from a big muscle beneath them, called the diaphragm. When it tightens, air rushes into your chest (and lungs). Relaxing it reduces the space in your chest, forcing you to breathe out.

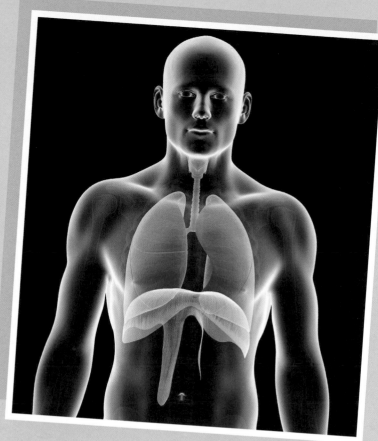

How long can some people hold their breath?

Some deep-sea divers can hold their breath for more than 20 minutes, but most people can manage only two minutes.

What's happening when we're out of breath?

Being out of breath is sometimes the sign of an illness, but usually it's because you've been exercising hard. That extra work for your muscles calls for increased oxygen, and sometimes your breathing can't keep pace. You need to stop and steady your breathing until you can continue with your exercise.

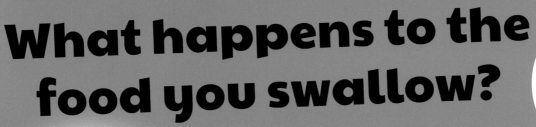

What happens to the food you swallow?

Burp!

You know that you need to eat food to provide your body with fuel and nutrients. But solid food—and also what you drink—isn't ready to help you right away. It needs to pass through your body and be digested. The digestive system is a series of long, twisting tubes that link your mouth and your stomach, and lead out through your anus (bottom) at the end.

Why do we burp?
We can easily swallow air along with our food, especially if we eat fast. That air escapes back the way it came in the form of a burp.

Why do we chew food?

Special chemicals called enzymes, contained in your saliva, start to break down what you've eaten. This sets off the process called digestion, or getting useful nutrients from what you eat. Chewing your food makes it easier for the enzymes to begin digesting it. Chewed food also travels more easily down to your stomach.

Why do astronauts eat from tubes?

Astronauts in space are weightless, and everything, including food, floats. Squeezing food from tubes is the best way to stop it from floating away.

Can you digest food if you're upside down?

Cartoons sometimes show food falling down a chute into the stomach. In reality, the food is squeezed from your mouth to your stomach. The tube that links them is surrounded by rings of muscles. They take turns to push the food along. And they work the same way whether you are upside down or the right way up!

How big is your stomach?

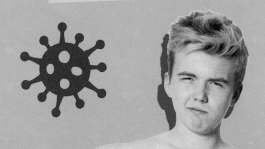

Well, it depends on your body size! The organ that is called the stomach is the size of a fist, but it doesn't take up the whole of your "tummy" space. The other parts of your digestive system sit in that space, too. The first stop is the stomach, then food moves on through the intestines.

Do you get a new stomach every few days?

In a way, you really do. The stomach has four layers, and the inner layer comes in contact with strong acids that break down food. That layer is constantly replaced, to protect the other layers (which include strong muscles) from those powerful acids.

Why does your tummy rumble sometimes?

Stomach muscles constantly squeeze food to break it up. Sometimes gases and air are squeezed out of the food... and rumble inside.

How much can your stomach stretch?

Your stomach is shaped like a letter J and has three main jobs: storing food, turning the food into more of a liquid, and sending it on to the small intestine. It needs to be stretchy for that first job, and your stomach can extend to 20 times its resting size after a big meal.

How long does food stay in your stomach?

It takes the stomach about three to four hours to break solid food down into a liquid mush called chyme. The chyme is then sent on to the intestines.

Is the small intestine really small?

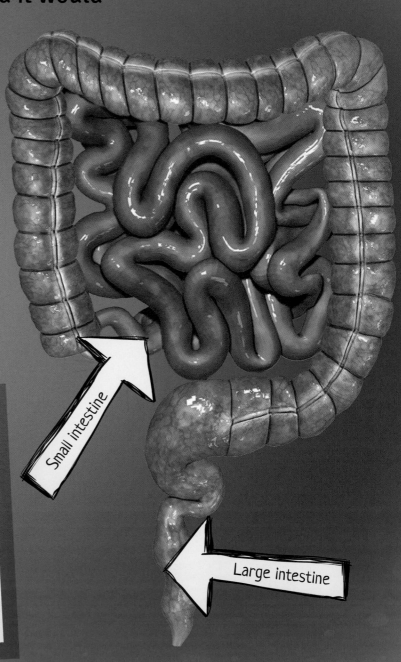

The small intestine is definitely not small in reality—uncoiled it would stretch out to 20 feet (6 m)! In fact, it is actually bigger than the large intestine. The intestines get their names from the width of their tubes: the small intestine is narrow and the large intestine is wide.

Small intestine

Large intestine

Can food travel up as well as down?

Valves called sphincters control the flow of food, making sure it keeps traveling down rather than coming back up through your esophagus.

How long does food spend in the intestines?

When food leaves the stomach it is nicely mashed up, but the body still needs to absorb all the nutrients. The small intestine spends around four hours breaking down the food and absorbing most of the vitamins and nutrients. The large intestine then spends an average of 40 hours filtering out water and any last nutrients before the remaining waste is ready to be expelled from the body.

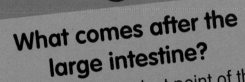

Ready, set, go!

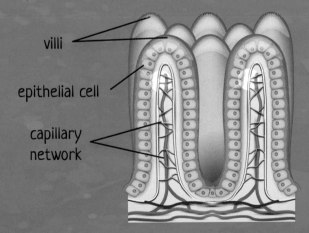

villi

epithelial cell

capillary network

What comes after the large intestine?

The rectum is the last point of the digestive system and is where food is held before being expelled out through the anus.

How does food pass out of the intestines?

The inside of the small intestine is covered in finger-like villi that increase the surface area. They are only one cell thick in places so food molecules can easily pass from the intestine into the blood-carrying capillaries running along the outside of the small intestine. The molecules are then carried around the body in the bloodstream.

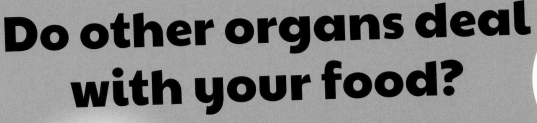

Do other organs deal with your food?

Many of your body's organs have more than one job to do. They need to help extract useful nutrients from your food while also producing important substances of their own. Some lesser-known organs, such as the pancreas and gallbladder, help the "stars" such as the stomach, liver, and intestines do their job.

Gallbladder

Pancreas

Yum!

What do we mean by rich food?

Rich food isn't food for rich people. It is food high in fats, such as butter and cream, that takes longer to digest.

20

Testing sugar levels is easy to do.

Does our body need sugar?

Too much sugar damages blood vessels but too little robs muscles and organs of fuel. Your pancreas monitors sugar levels in your body. It produces a chemical called insulin to deal with excess sugar and another called glucagon to tell your liver to produce more sugar if levels are low. Diabetes is a disorder where the pancreas cannot process sugar properly.

Why is human waste brown?

The liver produces a chemical called bile that helps digest fats. Extra bile is stored in an organ called the gallbladder. When bile reacts with bacteria in your guts, it turns the waste brown.

Why do we throw up?

Nausea—the sick feeling before you throw up—is a signal that your body needs to get rid of something harmful. Throwing up isn't nice, but you often feel better afterward, proving that it was necessary. Feeling sick is your body's way of giving you a message, just like an ache or pain stops you from using tired or damaged muscles.

Which is your busiest organ?

Your liver performs hundreds of jobs to keep your body working. You absolutely could not live without it—and it is so special that part of a liver can regrow into a whole one. The liver processes your food, stores the energy, gets rid of waste, and cleans your blood, as well as hundreds of other important tasks.

How are liver transplants special?

If you transplant part of a liver, it will grow to normal size in the sick person, and the bit left behind also grows back in the healthy person.

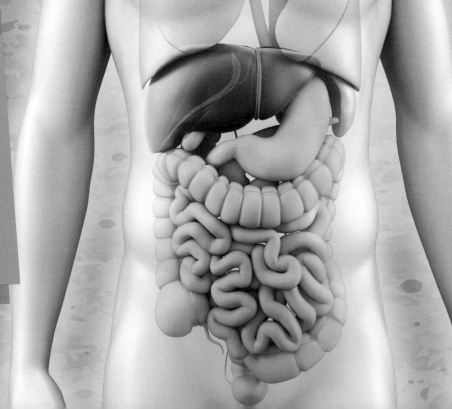

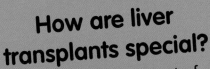

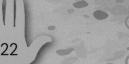

We're digesting!

How big is the liver?

It is the largest internal organ in the body, weighing about 3 pounds (1.4 kg). It grows as you do, reaching full size by about age 15: around 6 inches (15 cm) across. With more than 500 tasks to perform, from digesting food and breaking down toxins, to helping the blood clot, it's not surprising that the liver is so big.

What is the liver's most important job?

If you asked ten specialist doctors, you might get ten different answers, because the liver does so much. But the really vital job—sometimes needed to save your life—is to clean the poisons in your system. That's the liver's "emergency department" role, although the other 499 (or more) jobs are important.

What poisons does your liver deal with?

External poisons, such as drugs and alcohol, and ammonia, which is created internally by the body's everyday chemical reactions.

How are kidneys like filters?

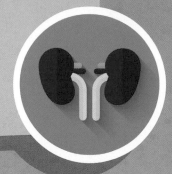

Your two fist-sized kidneys, located near the middle of your back, filter your blood to remove waste material and excess water. About 50 gallons (200 l) of blood pass through them each day. The blood comes out cleaner and the waste and water get sent off as urine.

Why is urine sometimes paler?

Urine contains different wastes along with water. Drinking lots of water reduces the concentration of wastes, making urine more watery, and clearer.

What if your kidneys don't work?

You could get by with one kidney, if the other became damaged. But losing a second kidney would cause serious problems because of the buildup of waste in your blood. Dialysis machines can take the place of kidneys, filtering blood and returning it to the patient's body.

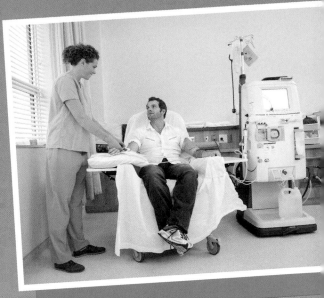

How do you know when you need to pee?

Urine gathers in an organ called the bladder. When it gets full, the bladder sends a message to your brain that it is emptying-out time!

Why are we so full of waste?

Your blood delivers nutrients around your body. Sometimes it brings stuff you already have enough of. Other stuff is broken down by chemical reactions in your cells, which can produce waste products—a bit like a car's exhaust. Water leaves your body as sweat, in your breath, and also in your poop, but the majority of it goes into your urine.

25

Do some organs just do nothing?

It might seem strange to think that your body carries around excess baggage that serves no purpose. But some parts of your body do seem to be souvenirs of a time when your ancestors—long ago—needed them to survive in very different conditions. Over time these body parts get smaller, but some never go away.

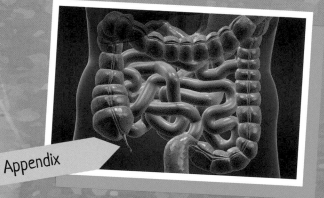

Appendix

What is your appendix for?

The appendix is a small tube attached to your large intestine. That's where your body digests food, except the human appendix doesn't seem to digest anything. Many scientists believe that it once helped human ancestors—like today's apes—to digest twigs and leaves.

Do your ears have muscles?

Your ears do have muscles to move them as monkeys do, except few people can "wiggle their ears" and use those muscles.

Do you really have a tail?

If you look behind any of your friends, you won't see any tail. But every human does have a tailbone, called the coccyx, at the base of the back. It's all that's left of a tail that our ancestors had millions of years ago—just as monkeys still have.

Do people have too many teeth?

The four "wisdom teeth" (molars) that develop when you're about 20 were most likely used by our ancestors to grind plants.

How does everything work together?

Our bodies are made up of different systems. Each system has its own function, such as converting food into energy, or removing waste. The systems all work together to bring the human body to life.

Circulatory system
Your heart is at the center of this system, which pumps blood around your body via veins and arteries.

Skeletal system
All 206 bones make up the skeletal system, which supports and protects your body.

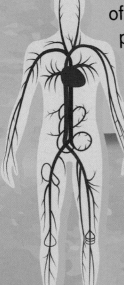

Muscular system
Around 640 muscles in your body help you move. Your muscles are attached to your bones by tendons.

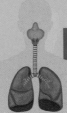

Respiratory system

Your lungs draw in air to bring oxygen into the body and push air out to move carbon dioxide out.

Nervous system

The brain passes messages around the body via a system of nerves. Nerves also pass messages received by your senses back to the brain.

Excretory system

Toxins and waste materials are removed from your body by this system, which includes your kidneys and bladder.

Testes (male)

Digestive system

This system takes in food, and breaks it down into energy and basic nutrients the body can use.

Endocrine system

Glands in this system produce chemicals called hormones that help you grow and change your mood.

Ovaries (female)

Glossary

acid A molecule with particular chemical properties and a pH of less than 7 used to digest food in the stomach.

artery A tube in the circulatory system that transports oxygenated blood from the heart around the body.

atrium One of the two chambers into which blood enters the heart.

bile A yellowish-brown fluid produced by the liver, stored in the gallbladder, that helps to break down fat.

capillary One of the smallest of the body's blood vessels.

carbon dioxide A colorless, odorless gas produced when the human body respires and breathes out.

cell The smallest functioning unit in an organism. Cells join together to make tissue.

diaphragm The muscle beneath the lungs that controls breathing.

energy The power to be active and perform jobs.

enzyme A special protein that helps chemical reactions occur.

esophagus The food pipe that connects the throat and the stomach.

fat A chemical substance that the body produces to store energy. It is stored in fat cells beneath the skin or surrounding organs.

glucagon A hormone made in the pancreas that acts in opposition to insulin to regulate blood glucose levels.

hormone A chemical that helps to regulate processes such as reproduction, growth and blood glucose levels.

insulin A hormone made in the pancreas that helps process glucose.

intestines The large and small intestines are the parts of the digestive system where nutrients are released from the food into the bloodstream.

kidneys The organs that filter waste products from the blood.

liver A major organ in the digestive system that has many jobs, including filtering the blood coming from the digestive system.

molecule The smallest possible unit of a substance that still behaves like that substance. A molecule is made up of two or more atoms.

nutrient Any substance that the body needs for energy or growth.

organ A collection of cells that work together to perform a specific function.

oxygen A colorless, odorless gas found in the air that the body breathes in.

protein One of the most important of all molecules in the body, protein is needed to strengthen and replace tissue in the body.

pulse The regular beat felt in the wrist or the neck as the heart pumps blood around the body.

tissue A collection of cells that look the same and have a similar job to do in the body.

valve A structure that allows fluid to move in one direction only by stopping it from flowing backwards.

veins Tubes in the circulatory system that transport deoxygenated blood from the body back to the heart.

ventricle One of the two chambers from which blood leaves the heart.

villi Fingerlike projections on the inside of the small intestine that allow the transfer of food molecules into the bloodstream.

Further Information

Further reading

The Complete Human Body *by Dr. Alice Roberts* (Dorling Kindersley, 2016)

Explore the Human Body *by Luann Columbo* (Canterbury Classics, 2016)

How Your Body Works: Getting Energy *by Philip Morgan* (Franklin Watts, 2011)

Mind Webs: Human Body *by Anna Claybourne* (Wayland, 2014)

Science in Action: Your Digestive System *by Sally Hewitt* (QED Publishing, 2016)

Your Body for Life: From Birth to Old Age *by Anne Rooney* (Raintree, 2013)

Websites

PowerKids Press has developed an online list of websites related to the subject of this book. This site is updated regularly. Please use this link to access the list: **www.powerkidslinks.com/hbfaq/heart**

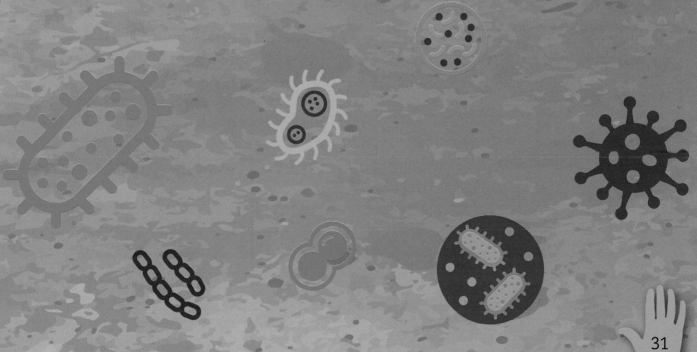

Index

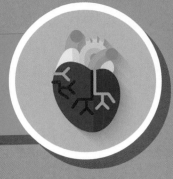

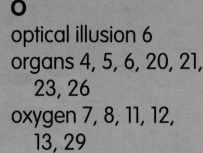